Finale
(Level 6)

Music & Materials by
Jennifer Eklund

PIANO PRONTO PUBLISHING
PianoPronto.com

Piano Pronto: Finale

Jennifer Eklund

Copyright ©2006 by Piano Pronto Publishing, Inc. All Rights Reserved.

WARNING: The compositions, arrangements, text, and graphics in this publication are protected by copyright law. No part of this work may be duplicated or reprinted without the prior consent of the author.

ISBN 978-0-9818616-6-1

Printed in the United States of America

Piano Pronto Publishing, Inc.
PianoPronto.com

Finale

TABLE OF CONTENTS

KEYBOARD CONCERTO THEME *(Bach)* 3
B MAJOR SCALE 5
JOURNEY'S END *(Eklund)* 7
SONATINA IN C *(Clementi)* 11
TRÄUMEREI *(Schumann)* 15
CANON IN D *(Pachelbel)* 18
WINTER THEME NO. 3 *(Vivaldi)* 22
PIANO CONCERTO NO. 20 *(Mozart)* 26
PASTORALE *(Burgmüller)* 30
SICILIENNE *(Fauré)* 34
ECOSSAISE IN G *(Beethoven)* 39
AVE MARIA *(Schubert)* 42
EL CHOCLO *(Villoldo)* 46
ARIOSO IN G *(Bach)* 50
DREAMWEAVER *(Eklund)* 53
PRELUDE IN E MINOR *(Chopin)* 58
BALLADE *(Burgmüller)* 62
FAIRY TALE *(Kabalevsky)* 66
SONATINA IN A MINOR *(Jacoby)* 70
D-FLAT MAJOR SCALE 73
RAINDROP PRELUDE *(Chopin)* 74
SONATINA IN C *(Spindler)* 79

Welcome to Finale
Review Questions

Before you begin:

♪ The next piece was composed by _____.

♪ He composed during the _____ period of music history.

♪ This piece was originally written for: **piano** *or* **harpsichord**

♪ The next piece is written in the **key of** _____.

♪ Name the accidentals in the **key signature**: _____

♪ The **tempo marking** _____ means _____.

♪ A **concerto** is a piece written for a:

small ensemble *or* **soloist and orchestra**

♪ How many movements are there in a typical **concerto?** _____

♪ During a **concerto** the musicians:

always play together *or* **take turns playing**

♪ Name two other composers who were active during J.S. Bach's life:

_____

1. Pronto Prep

♪ *Play the examples below to help prepare for "Keyboard Concerto Theme."*

1. Keyboard Concerto Theme

J.S. Bach
Arr. Jennifer Eklund

Allegro

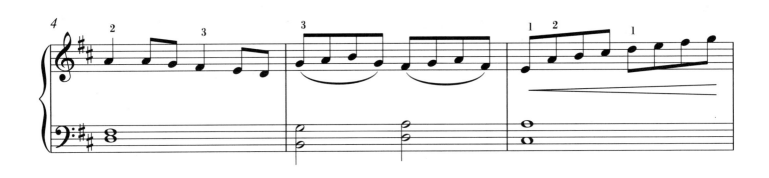
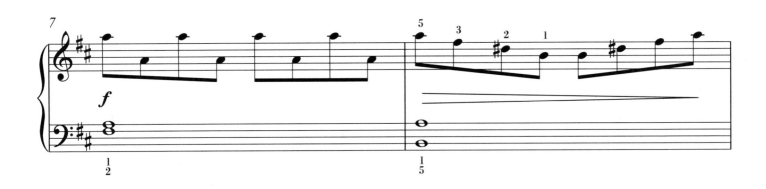

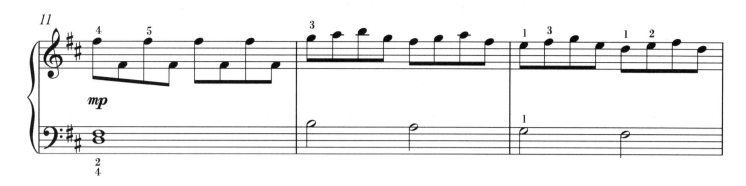
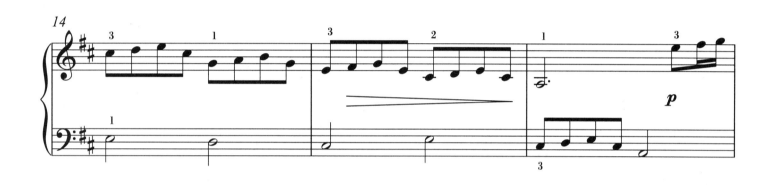
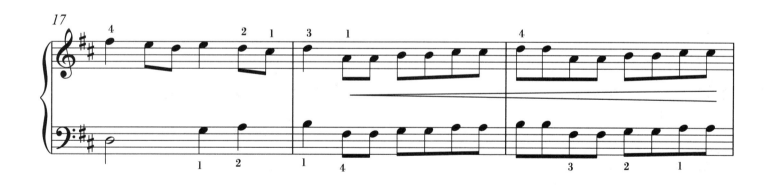
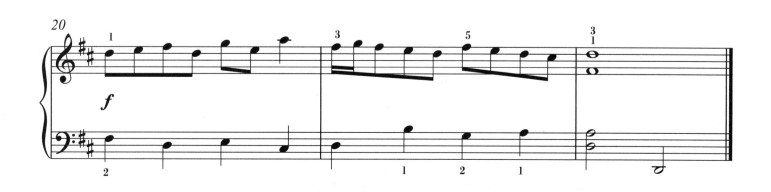

B Major

B Major Key Signature

All F's, C's, G's, D's, and A's are sharp.

B Major Scale

Practice playing the B major scale in each hand. Watch the fingerings!

Matching: Key Signature Review

A major	1 sharp
G major	3 sharps
D major	4 sharps
B major	5 sharps
E major	2 sharps

New Ending System

D.S. (*del segno*) = 𝄋 = the sign

Coda = ⊕ = ending

D.S. al Coda = play from the sign to the Coda

EXAMPLE SCORE

Follow the numberings on the score below to see how to use this ending system.

2. Journey's End

Jennifer Eklund

Copyright © 2006 Piano Pronto Publishing, Inc.
All Rights Reserved | PianoPronto.com

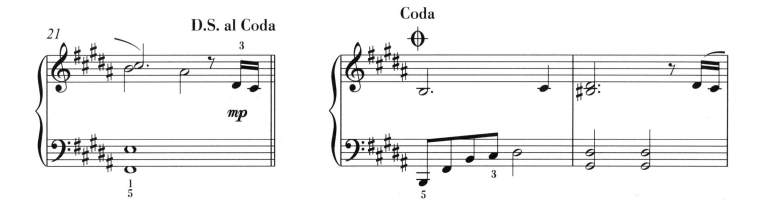

Sonata Form

Sonata form was widely used throughout the Classical period, and has a specific structure which you will learn about below. Keep in mind that sonata form was used in a wide variety of genres, from solo instrument works, to symphonies and other ensemble music.

Basic Layout of Sonata Form

Exposition

Most of the melodic material is introduced in the home key of the piece. There is always a repeat sign at the end of this section.

Development

The melodic themes that were introduced in the exposition are developed further. It is common for there to be many key changes in this section.

Recapitulation

The themes that were introduced in the exposition are brought back to complete the movement. There can be minor changes made to the material in this section.

Optional: Coda

Composers often included a final section known as the coda (remember that coda means ending in Italian). The purpose of the coda is to briefly introduce new themes or to lengthen the ending of a movement. Beethoven was particularly fond of writing long codas. In fact some of his codas actually contain more measures than the rest of the entire movement they are attached to!

Now It's Your Turn

Let's put our new knowledge to use and analyze the next piece, "**Sonatina in C.**"

♪ The **exposition** starts at measure _____ and ends at **measure** _____.

♪ The **development** starts at measure _____ and ends at **measure** _____.

♪ The **recapitulation** starts at measure _____ and ends at **measure** _____.

3. Pronto Prep

♪ *Play the examples below to help prepare for "Sonatina in C."*

3. Sonatina in C

Allegro   Muzio Clementi

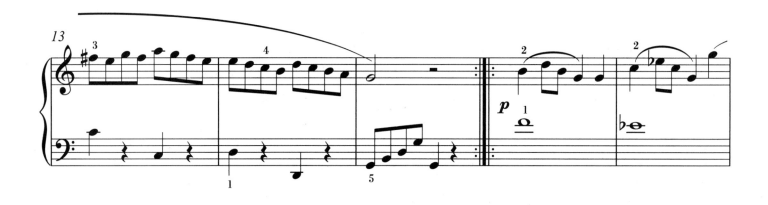

Key Review

MATCHING EXERCISE

    F major   *relative minor is* _____ *minor*

    C major   *relative minor is* _____ *minor*

    D major   *relative minor is* _____ *minor*

    A major   *relative minor is* _____ *minor*

    G major   *relative minor is* _____ *minor*

    E♭ major   *relative minor is* _____ *minor*

    B♭ major   *relative minor is* _____ *minor*

4. Pronto Prep

♫ *Play the examples below to help prepare for "Träumerei."*

Before you begin:

♫ The next piece is written in the **key of** _____.

♫ Robert Schumann (1810-1856) composed during the _____ period.

4. Träumerei
Dreaming

Robert Schumann
Arr. Jennifer Eklund

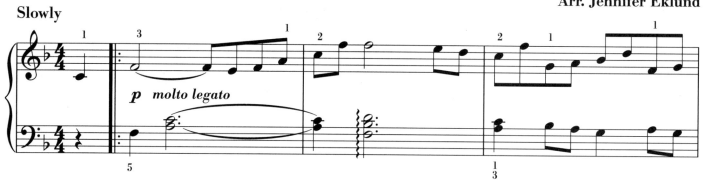
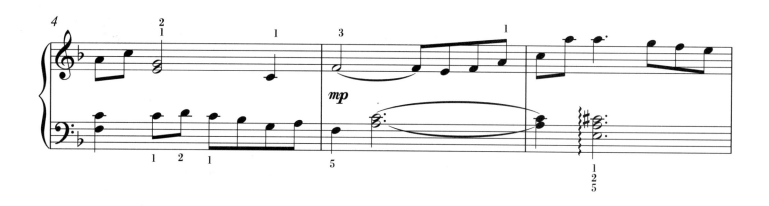

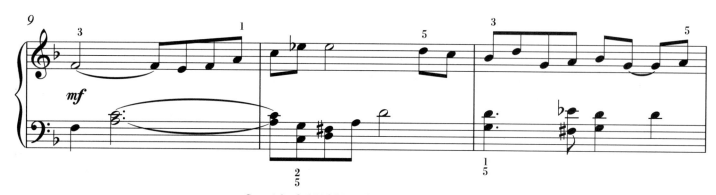

5. Pronto Prep

♪ *Play the examples below to help prepare for "Canon in D."*

Before you begin:

♪ The next piece is written in the **key of** _____.

♪ In this key all _____ and _____ are _____.

♪ Johann Pachelbel (1653-1706) composed during which period of music?

Classical *or* **Baroque**

♪ Name two other composers who composed during this period:

_____

5. Canon in D

Johann Pachelbel
Arr. Jennifer Eklund

Andante

6. Pronto Prep

♪ *Play the examples below to help prepare for "Winter Theme No. 3."*

6. Winter Theme No. 3

Antonio Vivaldi
Arr. Jennifer Eklund

Allegro

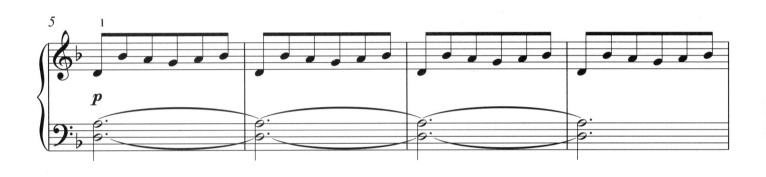
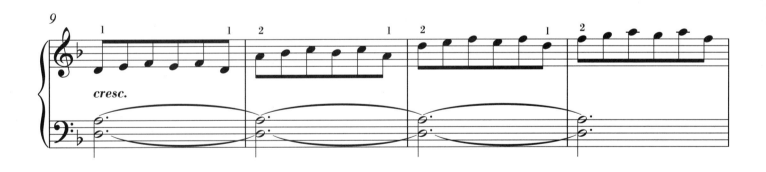

Copyright © 2006 Piano Pronto Publishing, Inc.
All Rights Reserved | PianoPronto.com

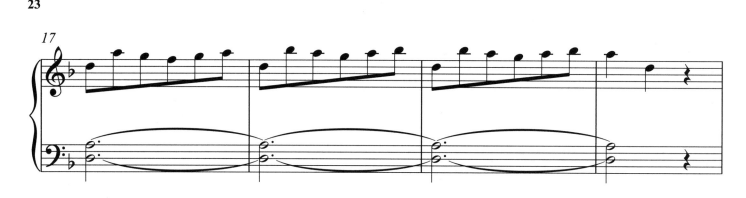
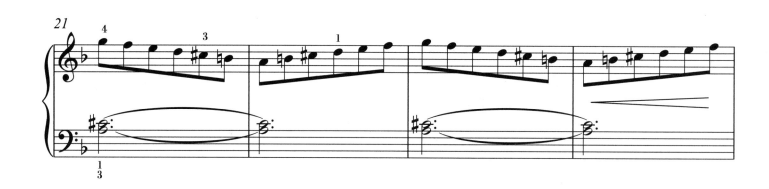

7. Pronto Prep

♪ *Play the examples below to help prepare for "Piano Concerto No. 20."*

7. Piano Concerto No. 20
Movement 2 Theme

W.A. Mozart
Arr. Jennifer Eklund

Andante

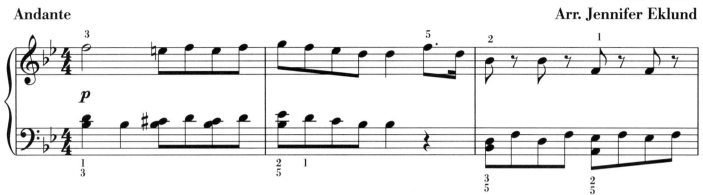

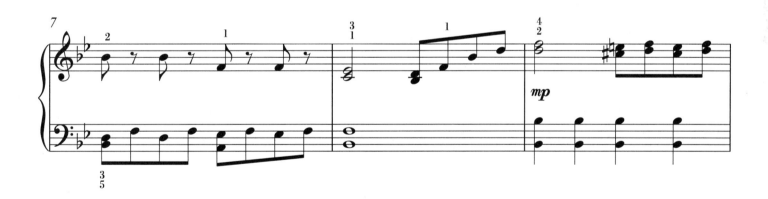

Copyright © 2006 Piano Pronto Publishing, Inc.
All Rights Reserved | PianoPronto.com

Grace Notes

The next piece uses **grace notes,** which are ornamental notes usually played quickly before the beat. Since there are many variations of grace notes, often related to the period of music during which the music was composed, the score will usually indicate in a footnote or the foreword how to play the grace notes.

Now It's Your Turn

The music below appears in the next piece you will play. The grace notes (*the small notes before the C*) should be played quickly before the beat.

8. Pronto Prep

♪ *Play the examples below to help prepare for "Pastorale."*

8. Pastorale

Andante
Burgmüller

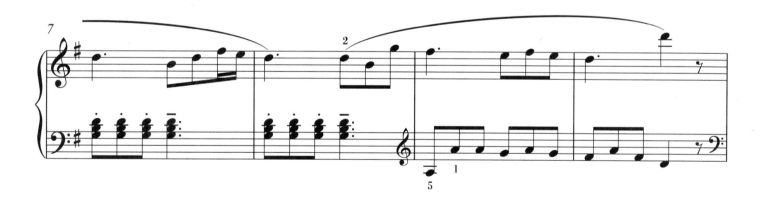
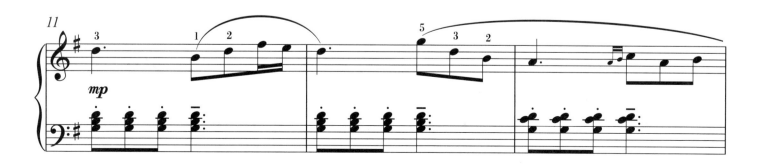

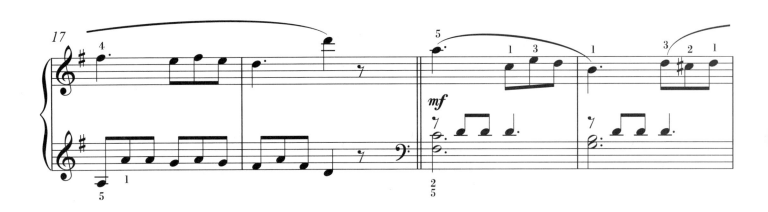
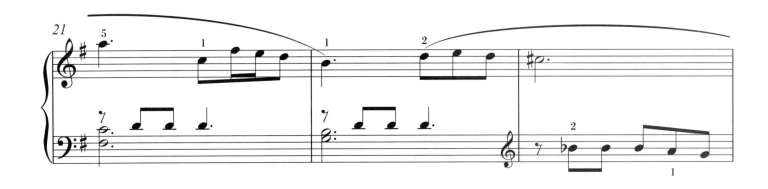
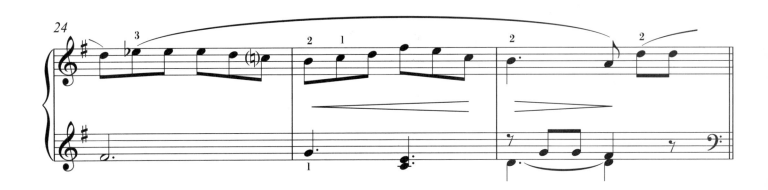

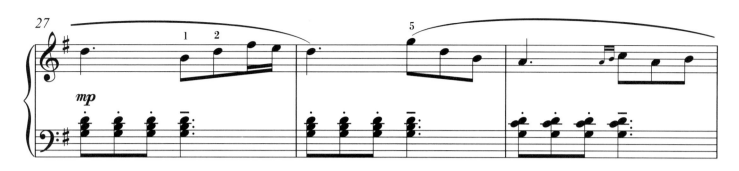
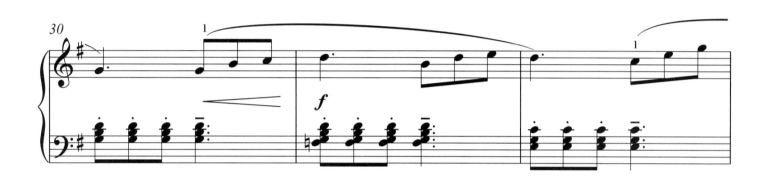

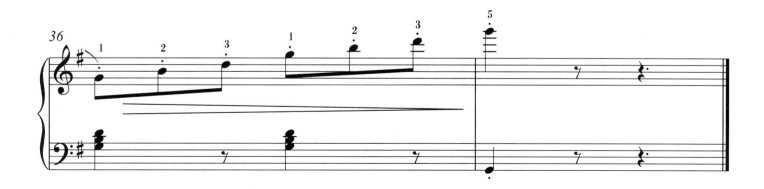

New Term

Andantino = a little slower than *Andante*

MATCHING: TEMPOS

Allegro con brio	Fast and playfully
Grazioso	Majestically
Scherzando	Gracefully
Maestoso	Humorously
Giocoso	Fast with animation
Moderato	Lightly and cheerfully
Andantino	Very slowly
Lento	Walking speed
Allegretto	Moderately
Andante	Slowly
Largo	Slower than *Andante*

9. Sicilienne

Gabriel Fauré
Arr. Jennifer Eklund

Andantino

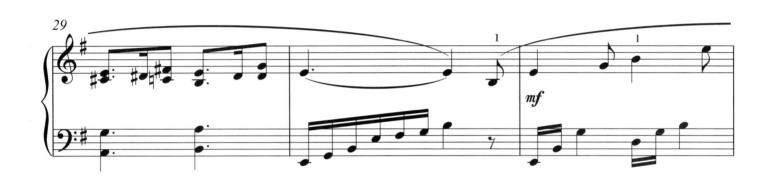

Major Key Review

Key Name	Number of accidentals	Name the accidentals
G major	1 sharp	F♯
D major		
F major		
A major		
B♭ major		
E major		
E♭ major		
B major		
A♭ major		

10. Pronto Prep

♪ *Play the examples below to help prepare for "Ecossaise in G."*

Before you begin:

♪ The next piece is in the **key of** _____.

♪ What is the **form** of the next piece?   **binary**   *or*   **ternary**

10. Ecossaise in G

Allegretto   Beethoven

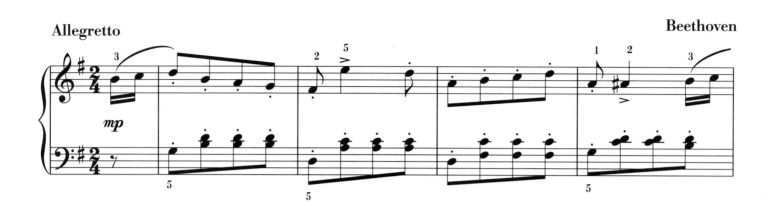
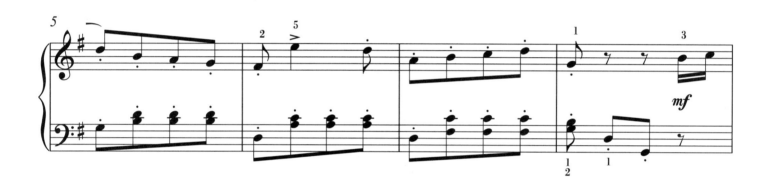
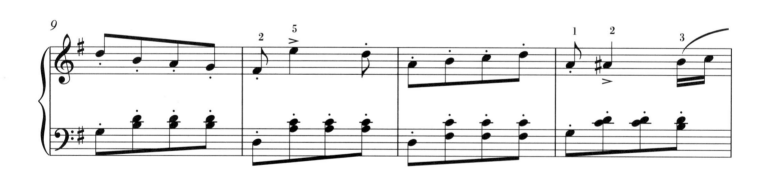

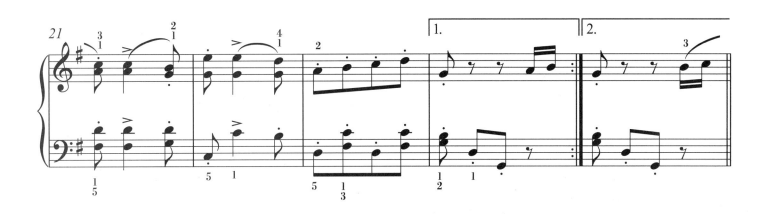

New Term

calando = gradually slower and softer

MATCHING: EXPRESSIONS

accelerando	gradually slower and softer
ritardando	gradually louder
crescendo	gradually slower
diminuendo	little by little
calando	gradually softer
poco a poco	gradually faster

Before you begin:

♪ Which hand plays the melody throughout the piece? _____

♪ Franz Schubert (1797-1828) composed during which period of music?

       Classical   *or*   **Romantic**

♪ Name two other composers who composed during this period:

_____

11. Ave Maria

Franz Schubert
Arr. Jennifer Eklund

Flowing

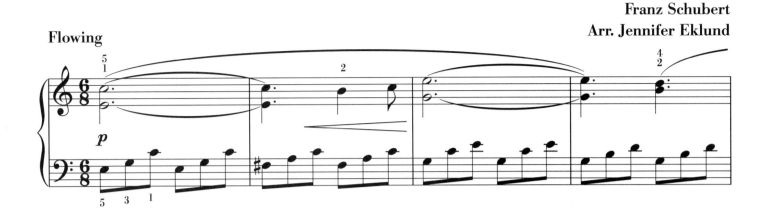
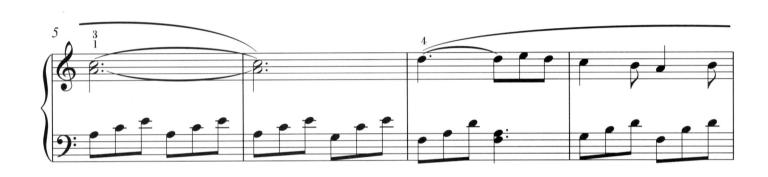
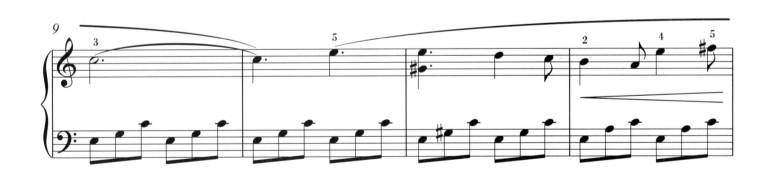

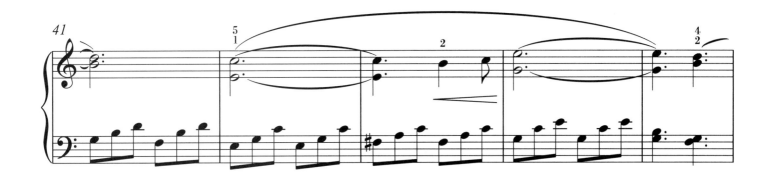

Minor Key Review

Key Name	Number of accidentals	Name the accidentals
D minor	1 flat	B♭
G minor		
F minor		
E minor		
F♯ minor		
C minor		
C♯ minor		
B minor		
G♯ minor		

12. El Choclo

A.G. Villoldo
Arr. Jennifer Eklund

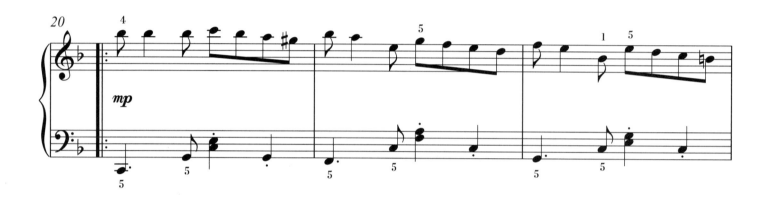
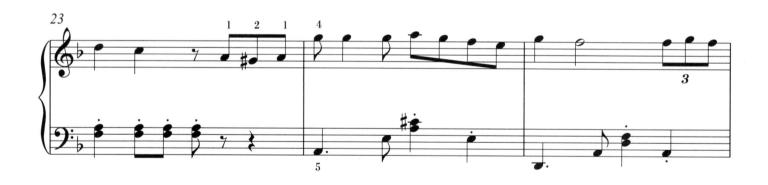

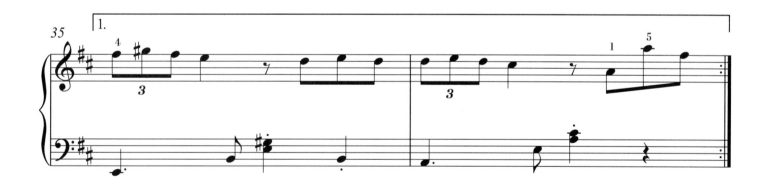

13. Pronto Prep

♪ *Play the examples below to help prepare for "Arioso in G."*

13. Arioso in G

J.S. Bach
Arr. Jennifer Eklund

Largo

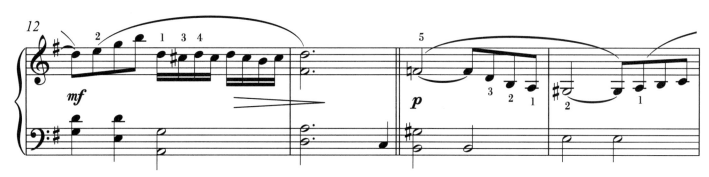

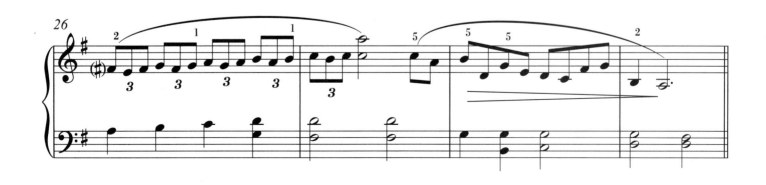

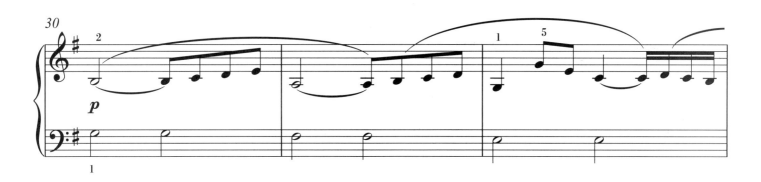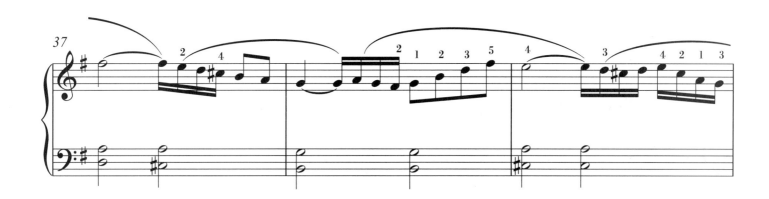

14. Dreamweaver

Flowing, but not fast

Jennifer Eklund

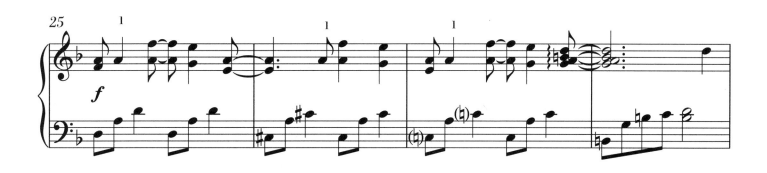

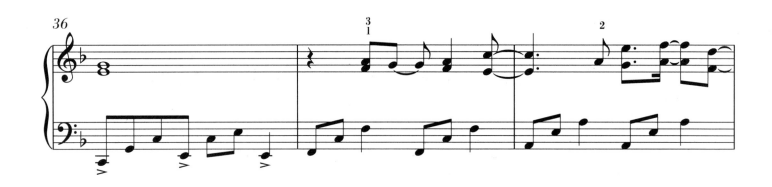

New Terms

rubato = Robbing time. Performer may slow down or speed up at will, as long as the basic meter is not changed. This technique is used most often in music of the Romantic period.

smorzando = fading away

15. Pronto Prep

♪ *Follow the directions below to help prepare for "Prelude in E Minor."*

- Play the entire piece with just the left hand. If you encounter unfamiliar notes, feel free to write in the letter names.

- Play the entire piece with the left hand once again, but try adding the **rubato** by speeding up and slowing down during each measure. Remember you have a lot of freedom with this technique—just make sure you still keep four beats per measure.

- Play the piece with just the right hand and write in any unfamiliar note names.

- Play the piece with just the right hand once again, playing as expressively as you can. The slurs mark where phrases begin and end; try to make the melody sing.

- When you feel comfortable, play the piece with both hands, watching all of the dynamic markings and articulations.

- Find the **smorzando** marking and circle it.

- **Frédéric Chopin (1810-1849)** composed during which period of music history?

15. Prelude in E Minor

Frédéric Chopin
Arr. Jennifer Eklund

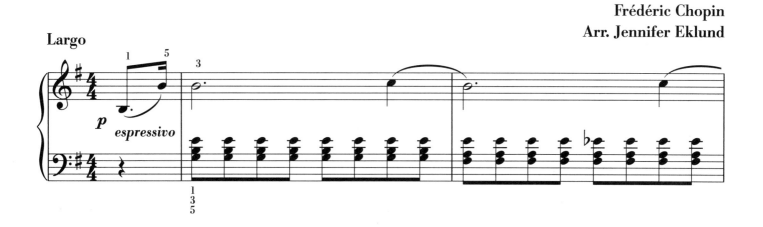

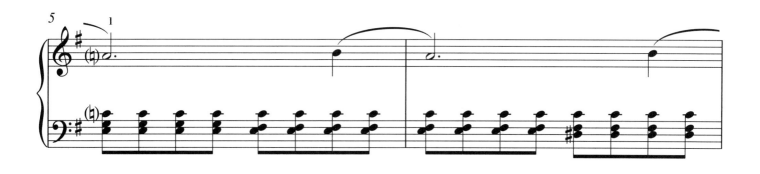

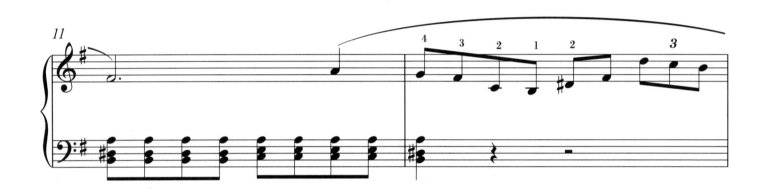
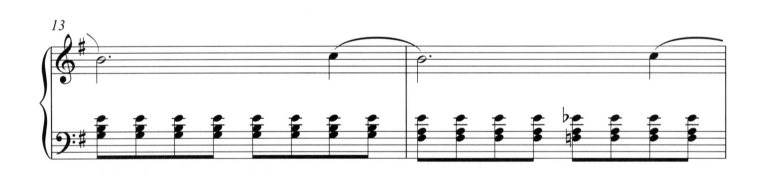

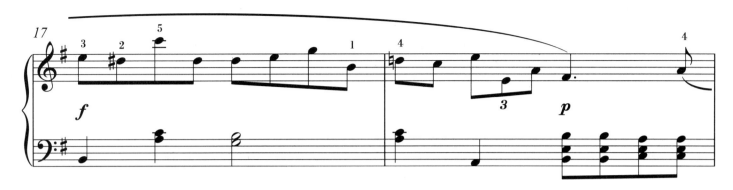

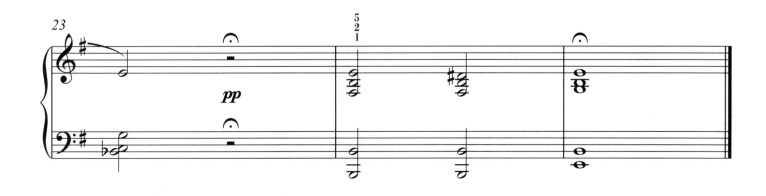

New Ending System

D.C. (*da capo*) = the beginning

Coda = ⊕ = ending

D.C. al Coda = play from the beginning to the Coda

Before you begin:

♪ Explain the **ending system** as it is used in the next piece.

♪ The next piece is written in the **key of** _____.

♪ Name the accidentals in the **key signature**: _____

♪ **Allegro con brio** means _____.

♪ What is the **form** of the piece?

        ternary   *or*   **ternary with coda**

♪ Which hand plays the melody on the first page? _____

♪ At **measure 31** the key changes to _____.

♪ What is the **time signature**? Explain what it means.

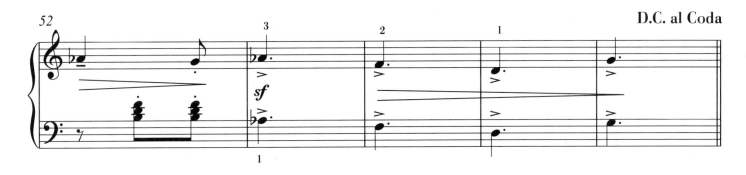

D.C. al Coda

The Contemporary Period
(1900–Today)

The Contemporary period in music is an era of wide variety. At the turn of the 20th century, composers were moving toward highly dissonant sounds while rejecting formal ideas of the past eras. Pop music, including jazz, blues, and rock and roll, are also important genres that have continued to evolve and grow in popularity.

Important Piano Composers

- **Arnold Schoenberg** – (1874-1951)
- **Béla Bartók** – (1881-1945)
- **George Gershwin** – (1898-1937)
- **Duke Ellington** – (1899-1974)

Musical Style of the Contemporary Period

- Anything goes—melody, harmony, and formal techniques are stretched to their limits.

- Dissonant sounds are widely used, accepted, and embraced as a part of concert music.

- Starting as early as the 1920s, jazz was being played and developed in the lower class neighborhoods of New York City and Chicago. Jazz was not widely accepted as a *high art* form and usually not performed on traditional concert stages. George Gershwin and Duke Ellington were two American composers who successfully mixed jazz and concert forms together and had their music performed in traditionally classical venues.

Keyboard Music of the Contemporary Period

- The musicians and composers of this era experimented with all the differing sounds that the piano can output. Composers developed the use of overtones, and some compositions required the pianist to play on the strings instead of the keys,

- John Cage invented the "prepared piano" in which everyday items such as paper clips, pencils, etc., were placed on the strings inside the piano in order to create a variety of percussive sound effects.

- In the world of jazz music the piano was a primary instrument used in nearly every type of performance ensemble.

17. Fairy Tale

Andantino
Kabalevsky

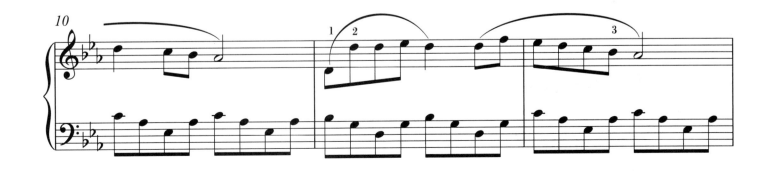

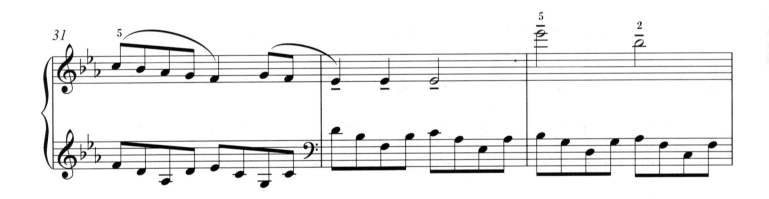

18. Pronto Prep

♪ *Play the examples below to help prepare for "Sonatina in A Minor."*

Before you begin:

♪ The next piece is in the **key of** _____.

♪ List the **three sections** of a sonatina movement below. Describe them.

_____

_____

_____

♪ Find and label these sections in the next piece.

18. Sonatina in A Minor

Russell Jacoby

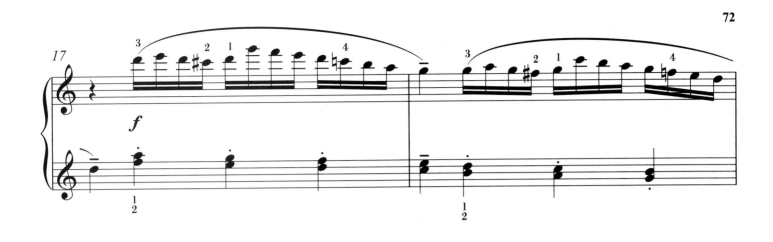

D♭ Major

D♭ Major Key Signature

All B's, E's, A's, D's, and G's are flat.

D♭ Major Scale

Practice playing the D♭ major scale in each hand. Watch the fingerings!

Matching: Key Signature Review

F major	2 flats
E♭ major	5 flats
B♭ major	1 flat
A♭ major	3 flats
D♭ major	4 flats

19. Raindrop Prelude

Frédéric Chopin
Arr. Jennifer Eklund

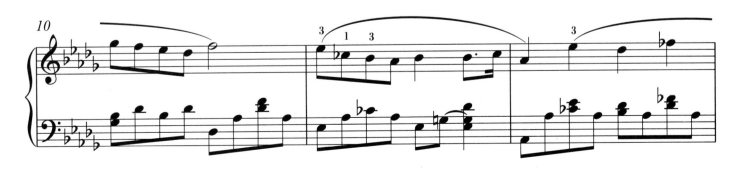

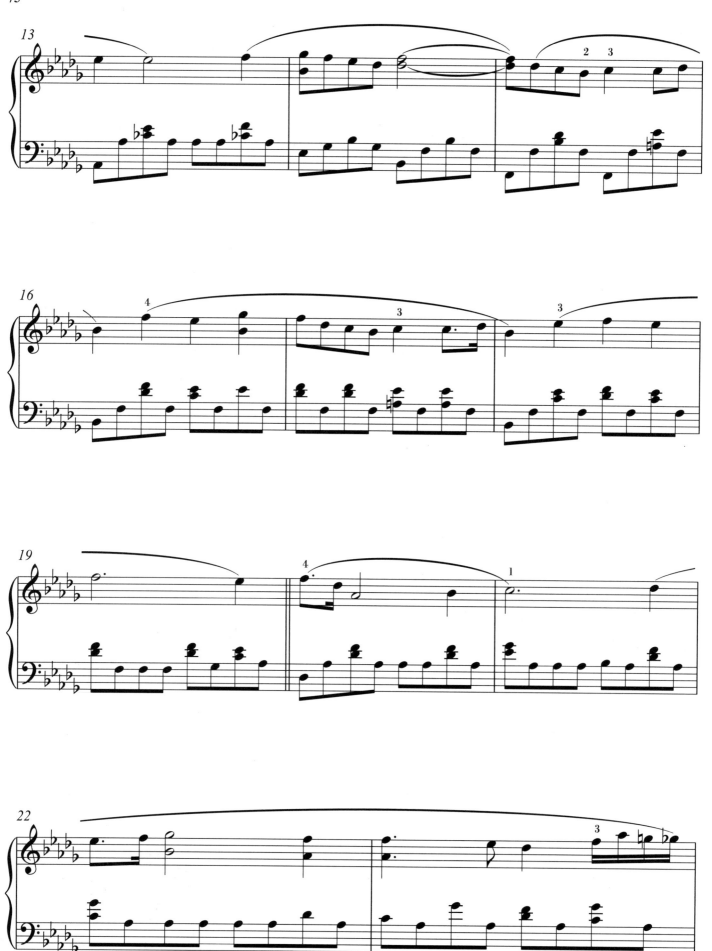

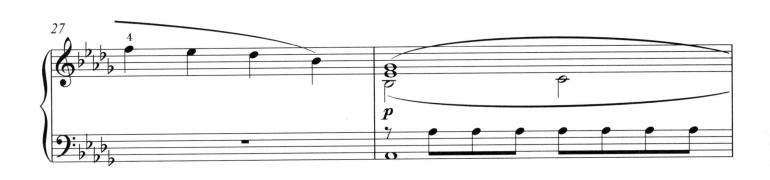

Final Review Questions

Before you begin:

♪ How many **movements** are in the next piece? _____

♪ List the **three sections** of a sonatina movement below. Describe them.

_____

_____

_____

♪ Find and label these section in both movements. (*Hint: look for repeat signs.*)

♪ The **tempo** of the first movement is _____ which means _____.

♪ The **tempo** of the second movement is _____ which means _____.

♪ In the second movement how do you play the right hand notes in mm. 13-16?

cross under the left hand   *or*   **cross over the left hand**

♪ In the second movement there is a **key change** at m. 29 to _____.

♪ Does the first movement have a **coda**? If so, where does it start? _____

♪ Does the second movement have a **coda**? If so, where does it start? _____

20. Pronto Prep

♪ *Play the examples below to help prepare for "Sonatina in C."*

20. Sonatina in C
Movement 1

Allegro
Fritz Spindler

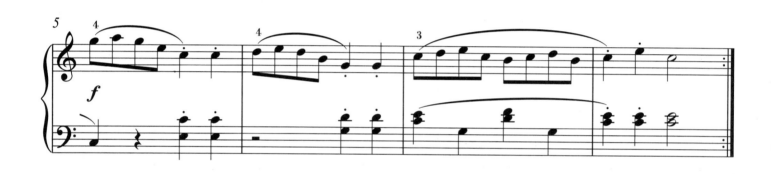
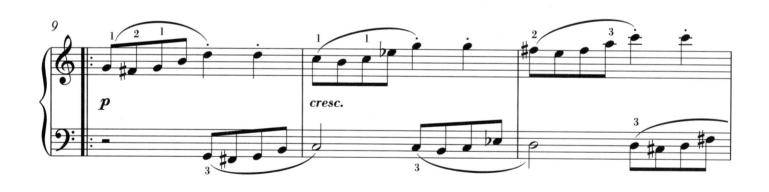

Movement 2

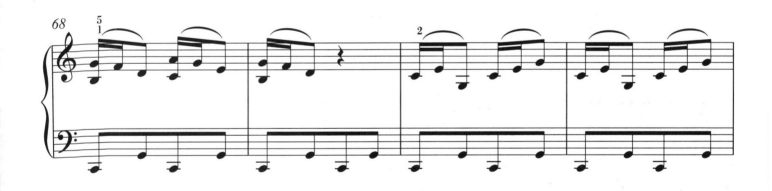